Praise for
Face to Face with Jesus

"This is a small book that will have a big impact on your life. Archbishop Bruno Forte combines the knowledge of a theologian with the passion of a devoted disciple to create a book that is a must-read for any believer. You'll encounter Christ in a deeper, more personal way after walking through the Gospel of Mark with Archbishop Forte."

— Jennifer Fulwiler, author of ConversionDiary.com

"Archbishop Forte's spiritual interpretation of the Gospel of Mark is informed by historical and literary insights as well as the stages of spiritual growth that call for conversion, right choice, and loving union with God. By reading the story as an initiation into the life-long journey of faith for catechumens, Archbishop Forte provides a valuable pastoral resource for RCIA and Adult Faith Formation groups."

— Pheme Perkins, PhD, professor of theology, Boston College

"In *Face to Face with Jesus*, Archbishop Bruno Forte, an outstanding theologian and preacher, opens up the Gospel of Mark in a way that helps readers discover—through the eyes of the first followers of Jesus—the Christian way of life. We are invited into a guided spiritual exercise by a master catechist who welcomes those who feel their relationship with Jesus may have grown cold or could be stronger to rediscover the fire of their faith. In *Face to Face with Jesus*, the Gospel of Saint Mark comes alive as a manual of Christian living for all those seeking to know the fullest expression of human love found only in the Risen Lord."

— Cardinal Donald Wuerl, Archbishop of Washington, DC

FACE TO FACE WITH JESUS

FACE TO FACE WITH JESUS

Reflections for a Disciple

Bruno Forte

With a foreword by Scott Hahn

BOOKS & MEDIA
Boston

Library of Congress Cataloging-in-Publication Data

Forte, Bruno.
  [Ma voi, chi dite che io sia? English]
  Face to face with Jesus : reflections for a disciple / Bruno Forte ; with a foreword by Scott Hahn.
       pages cm
  ISBN-13: 978-0-8198-2723-4
  ISBN-10: 0-8198-2723-1
  1. Bible. Mark--Criticism, interpretation, etc. I. Title.
  BS2585.52.F6713 2014
  226.3'0709--dc23

                                        2013029408

Originally published by Edizioni San Paolo, Milan in Italian as *Ma voi, chi dite che io sia?: In cammino con Gesù nel Vangelo di Marco.*

Translated by Bret Thoman

Cover design by Rosana Usselmann

Cover art by D. Buoninsegna, Jesus Opens Eyes of a Man Born Blind

Published by Pauline Books & Media, 50 Saint Pauls Avenue, Boston, MA 02130-3491. www.pauline.org

Printed in the U.S.A.

Pauline Books & Media is the publishing house of the Daughters of St. Paul, an international congregation of women religious serving the Church with the communications media.

1 2 3 4 5 6 7 8 9   18 17 16 15 14

This little book contains the meditations of the "spiritual exercises for everyone" that I gave to a large and attentive crowd over the course of three evenings during Lent of 2012 in a large church in Chieti, Italy. I dedicate the following pages to those listeners, as well as to all who will imitate them in their desire to walk with Jesus in the Gospel of Mark.

Contents

Foreword

Long before I was a theologian—and even before I called myself a Christian—I was a musician. Though I spoke not a word of Italian, I knew the word *forte* because it appeared often on sheet music. To a musician, *forte* means strong, bold, loud. You see it on music that aims to make an impression.

It's a word that suits this book and its author. Archbishop Bruno Forte is an eminent churchman, a world-renowned scholar, and a passionate Christian man.

His zeal is evident in his manifold accomplishments. He holds doctorates in both philosophy and theology, and he has taught in both disciplines at prestigious universities throughout Europe. He is a prolific author, best known for his eight-volume *Simbolica Ecclesiale* and four-volume *Dialogica*. For a solid decade he served on the Church's

International Theological Commission, the elite group of theologians who advise the Holy See in doctrinal matters of major importance. He was one of the founding members of the Pontifical Council for Promoting the New Evangelization. Since 2004 he has been Archbishop of Chieti-Vasto in Italy.

He is a scholar of the first rank, but before he is a scholar, he is a pastor, and before he is a pastor, he is a disciple. Yet these various roles do not divide his life. I know him only through his work, but his words are the product of a remarkably integrated life. He writes with the depth of a man who has spent long years in research, but also with the passion of a preacher who spends hours on his knees in prayer. In the pages of his work, he seems to say to us the words that the disciples said at Emmaus: "Did not our hearts burn within us while he talked to us on the road, while he opened to us the scriptures?" (Lk 24:32 RSV).

Archbishop Forte is a scholar unashamed of his love for Jesus Christ. It is Jesus who has inspired the man to earn two doctorates and write so many books. Archbishop Forte is the rare scholar who cannot help but use exclamation points when he discusses matters of divine revelation. "God Speaks!" he proclaims in a subheading in one of his pastoral letters—as if the fact would be ill-served by an unadorned declarative sentence.

That pastoral letter, written in 2006, bore an evocative title: "The Word for Living: Sacred Scripture and the Beauty of God." It is a rich document, written to address what the Archbishop recognizes as a postmodern crisis, a longing that is frustrated and unfulfilled. God permits this for a reason, he explains, quoting the Prophet Amos: "'Behold, the days are coming,' says the Lord GOD, 'when I will send a famine on the land; not a famine of bread, nor a thirst for water, but of hearing the words of the LORD'" (Amos 8:11 RSV). The Archbishop continues:

> I recognize this hunger in the need for love that is in each of us, men and women of this postmodern time. We are becoming more and more prisoners of our solitude. Only an infinite love can satisfy the expectation that burns inside of us: Only the God who is love can say to us that we are not alone in this world, and that our house is in the heavenly city where there will no longer be neither sorrow nor death. "From that city," writes Augustine, "our Father has sent us letters, he has sent us the Scripture, and from this awakens our desire to return home."[1]

For Archbishop Forte, those letters from our Father are not simply historical artifacts. They are life's blood—a

---

1. Bruno Forte, "The Word for Living: Sacred Scripture and the Beauty of God Pastoral Letter for 2006–2007," no. 1. Last accessed June 2013 at http://www.zenit.org/en/articles/archbishop-bruno-forte-on-scripture.

transfusion of divine life. They are as "living and active" (Heb 4:12) today as they were the day they were written. Our Father inspired them for each of us—for you and for me—as if we would be their only reader or listener.

He speaks this way of the entirety of Scripture, both the Old Testament and the New. For the Archbishop, as for the sacred authors, it's all about Christ; and it's not merely about him in the way a biography is about its subject. "It shares his power," [2] Archbishop Forte exclaims. The words of Scripture are revelations from God, so they provide knowledge we could not attain through our own efforts (even if we were to earn two doctorates). The words of Scripture are inspired by God; he breathes them into being as surely as he breathed life into Adam.

The words of Scripture share God's power, especially when they are encountered in the Church—in catechesis, in study, but especially in liturgy. It is in the Church's worship that the Word comes to us with sacramental power—with *his* power. In the liturgy, the Word is made flesh and dwells among us, and we are made partakers of that flesh.

What Archbishop Forte said in general terms about Scripture in his pastoral letter, he applies here to a

---

2. Ibid, no. 2.

particular book of the Bible, the Gospel According to Saint Mark.

Face to Face with Jesus is a personal and pastoral book, a series of brief spiritual exercises intended to move us to a deeper encounter with Jesus, by means of *lectio divina*—disciplined, prayerful consideration of the Word of God.

It is a work, like the Lord's own preaching, capable of reaching the hearts and minds of multitudes. It is the fruit of deep prayer. Yet it is also the fruit of decades of careful scholarship and academic engagement.

The Archbishop knows that most people go to the Bible because they want to find its spiritual sense. But he knows, too, that the spiritual sense of Scripture rests on the foundation of the literal-historical sense: *historia fundamentum est*. God entered history at a particular time and place, among a certain people, and said and did specific things. The Word took flesh. Thus, all our spiritual interpretation of Scripture must be grounded in literal and historical facts.

And so Archbishop Forte helps us to understand the ancient catechetical form and purpose of each of the four gospels. Saint Mark's presents a manual for the catechumen, for those members of the primitive communities who were beginning their journey—their walk with Jesus, as we see in the subtitle of this book.

As a result, this is an informative book, but more importantly it is a *formative* book. A pastor and spiritual director—who is himself an intentional disciple of Jesus—has taken us into his tutelage. That is our privilege. One of the Church's masters of evangelization is evangelizing us, and he is doing so with a proven instrument. Mark's Gospel succeeded quite well in its work of evangelizing and catechizing the Church's first generation, and it speaks with the same power—divine power—to our own generation.

When we read the evangelists the right way, we never cease to be evangelized. Conversion is thus life long and daily, as Jesus—the living Word who proclaims the Evangel through the evangelists—leads us along the ways of the interior life, from purification, all the way through illumination, to communion.

That is the way we walk in the course of this book, with a spiritual guide who is strong, bold: *Forte*.

Scott Hahn

Preface

This is a small book. It is the kind that is held in the palms of your hands, as Edmond Jabès has said:

> "Do you know why our books of wisdom and of prayers are small?" the master asked his disciple. "Because they are books that contain a secret, and a secret should not be disclosed. Prudence of the soul. Love is expressed quietly. The book of our masters is the size of our hands, open only for us."[1]

Opened toward heaven! And this is how this small book should be read, because it is a type of "spiritual exercises" for all people and for each person in particular.

---

1. Edmond Jabès, *Uno straniero con, sotto il braccio, un libro di piccolo formato*, trans. A. Folin (Milano: SE, 1991), 19.

The spiritual exercises are explained very well by the one who gave them their definitive form in the history of Christian spirituality: Saint Ignatius of Loyola. He writes at the beginning of his book (also small!):

> By the term, spiritual exercises, is meant every way of examining one's conscience, of meditating, of contemplating, of praying vocally and mentally, and of performing other spiritual actions . . . diverse means to prepare and dispose the soul to rid itself of all disordered affections, and, after eliminating them, to seek and find the will of God in the management of one's life for the salvation of the soul.[2]

The objective of the spiritual exercises is, therefore, "to conquer oneself and regulate one's life" (no. 21), in order to realize always more the destination for which we were created, "to praise, reverence, and serve God our Lord" (no. 23). For this reason, the pathway of the exercises involves three main stages, so important also to the great spiritual tradition: the purgative way, the illuminative way, and the unitive way.

The first stage, the purgative way, indicates a change of heart and of life: *deformata reformare*. This consists in decisively reforming that which separates us from God. It directs us to verify our choices in the plan that the eternal

---

2. *Spiritual Exercises,* First Annotation.

Lord has for us: "Whoever follows me will never walk in darkness but will have the light of life" (Jn 8:12).

The purpose of the second stage, the illuminative way, is to conform one's heart and life to the living God: *reformata conformare* being the Latin expression according to the spiritual tradition. In this stage, one enters into the experience of contemplative prayer and listens to the word of God while walking in the ways of silence.

Finally, the third stage, the unitive way, helps us to become partakers of divine life given from above. This stage bears full fruit in the conversion of heart and in striving for holiness according to the plan that the Father has for each of us: *conformata confirmare*. This confirms the divine work in our hearts and in our lives with the seal of the Holy Spirit.

These exercises, set out here in a simple and essential format, accompany Jesus of Nazareth, the Christ of God, through Mark's account. The reason for the choice of this particular Gospel will be explained in the following reflections. Suffice it to say here that Mark's Gospel (also a small book) presents itself as a type of manual for the catechumen, well suited to accompany those who desire and seek an encounter with Jesus.

It is precisely for this reason that the "spiritual exercises" that follow should be considered *for everyone*. They are for those who already believe and who desire to encounter the Lord of their life in an increasingly deeper and livelier way. Yet, they are also for inquiring non-believers who may want to get to know this Jesus of Nazareth and the choices that he made and proposed to us and to those who are open to a challenge and to what, I believe, is a promise for everyone.

B. F.
Easter, 2012

Why the Gospel of Mark?

The Gospel of Mark is the shortest and oldest of the four Gospels. It is sixteen chapters long, totaling 678 verses, and has been called the "Gospel of one night."[1] No one who reads it, even quickly, can be unaffected by the tension that runs through it, since it is concise and strongly engaging. First of all, the tension of the past runs through to the present; the account of the story of Jesus of Nazareth is created to speak to today's hearers, to whom it is presented. But there is also the tension between the present and the past, as if the questions of the present-day

---

1. See Benoît Standaert, *Marco: Vangelo di una notte, vangelo per la vita,* 3 vols (Bologna: EDB, 2011).

believer point to the origin of the faith. The earthly ministry of Jesus is told as the point of reference to which the
believer must turn in order to walk with the Son of Man /
Son of God on the journey from darkness to light. It is a
journey that repeats itself throughout the book in a spiral
of successive stages, concluding in the final profession of
the centurion at the foot of the cross, "Truly this man was
God's Son!" (Mk 15:39).

Just so, Mark's account presents itself as a *life journey*,
one that challenges and progresses, culminating in the
experience of the Risen One. Cardinal Carlo Maria Martini
writes:

> Mark presented a catechesis, a manual for the cate-
> chumen . . . for those members of the primitive
> communities who were beginning their catechume-
> nal journey. . . . Matthew's . . . is the Gospel of the
> catechist; that is, the Gospel which gives the catechist
> a number of doctrines, prescriptions, and exhorta-
> tions. Luke is the doctor's Gospel; that is, the Gospel
> for the one who wants an in-depth historical-salvific
> treatment of the mystery with a broader vision of it.
> Finally, John's is the Gospel of the priest, which gives
> the mature and contemplative Christian a unified
> vision of the various mysteries of salvation.
>
> Mark is the first of these four manuals . . . centered,
> therefore, on the catechumenal journey. It can be
> summed up in the words of Jesus to his disciples: "To

> you has been given the secret of the kingdom of God,
> but for those outside, everything comes in parables"
> (Mk 4:11).
>
> Mark's Gospel shows us how, through the para-
> bles, through the *exterior* scene of the mystery of the
> kingdom, we can enter *inside* it and receive this
> secret.[2]

It is a challenging journey, placing before us important
decisions to be made about our lives and our choices. In
this sense, the narrative of Mark is "like a play, where the
outcome is not obvious. . . . Each reader is invited to journey with the characters in the play both in their search for
the true identity of Jesus as well as in the discovery of his
or her own identity."[3] In this light, Peter—a central character in the story—appears as the voice of the catechumen,
who opens himself gradually, not without resistance, to
receive the revelation of the Son of God. "The Gospel of
Mark presents itself as the pathway of a journey ranging
from fear and doubt to the joy and peace of the encounter. . . . The drama of Jesus Christ is presented as the
parable to which every human being is called: to lose his

---

2. Carlo Maria Martini, *The Spiritual Journey of the Apostles: Growth in the Gospel of Mark*, trans. K.D. Whitehead (Boston: Pauline Books & Media, 1991), 7–8.

3. R. Fabris, *Marco* (Assisi: Cittadella Editrice, 2005), 14.

life in order to find it."[4] The road on which Jesus travels
from Galilee to Jerusalem is not, in short, a mere geographical and chronological route; rather, it is a journey
that can be considered symbolic. And it invites others to
follow as well.

Relating to this idea, one could affirm that in Mark's
account, Jesus presents his identity, as if veiled, in a *progressive journey*. He does so in order to propose not impose
himself on one's freedom to consent. At its culmination is
an affirmative profession of faith, proposed at the outset in
the title, "The beginning of the good news of Jesus Christ,
the Son of God" (Mk 1:1). The final profession is placed in
the mouth of a pagan, the Roman centurion, at the foot of
the cross, "Truly this man was God's Son!" (Mk 15:39).
The itinerary leading to this profession is made up of an
alternating series of revelations and secrets. This has been
called the messianic secret.[5] The term refers to the attitude
of Jesus during his public ministry of hiding his identity as
the Messiah. Sometimes he does so to the disciples (Mk
8:29–30), at times to those who received miracles (Mk 1:44;

---

4. Ibid., 15.

5. This term was coined by W. Wrede, *Il segreto messianico nei Vangeli*
(Napoli: D'Auria, 1995); originally in German: *Das Messiasgeheimnis
in den Evangelien* (1901; 1969). This book also exists in English: *The
Messianic Secret* (Lutterworth Press, 1987)

5:43; 7:36; 8:26), at other times to exorcised demons (Mk 1:25; 1:34; 3:12). In the end, Jesus openly declares his identity just as his passion begins and he is being forsaken by the crowd and by his disciples. He manifests himself openly as the Christ-Messiah, "Again the high priest asked him, 'Are you the Messiah, the Son of the Blessed One?' Jesus said, 'I am'" (Mk 14:61–62).

Mark offers what is, ultimately, a *paschal journey*: "The first part deals with a progressive recognition of who Jesus is. Then, once he is recognized, Jesus draws his disciples and followers to walk behind him, journeying along the road to the cross."[6] One may then ask how "this text was utilized in the community or communities that saw it come into existence."[7] At a literary level, the text contains all the hallmarks of a speech and a dramatic action that should be proclaimed all at once in the same breath. A suggested hypothesis is that Mark's account was read at night during the vigil of Easter between Holy Saturday and Resurrection Sunday. For some listeners, those who were new members of the community, such a night was the culmination of their Christian initiation. At the conclusion of the entire Gospel reading, they would be baptized and

---

6. Benoît Standaert, *Il Vangelo secondo Marco* (Roma: Borla, 1984), 43.

7. Standaert, *Marco, Vangelo di una notte, vangelo per la vita*, 3:7.

called to participate for the first time in the Eucharistic banquet. As the structure of the Jewish Passover meal included a dramatic account, the *haggadah* (narrative reading), which was the thread throughout the ritual, so the early Christian Easter Vigil would have offered a similar account: the Gospel of Mark. Benoît Standaert maintains: "After the reading of the Gospel of Mark, the people would go to the river or the sea to baptize the catechumens. Then they would gather together for the Eucharistic banquet celebrated early in the morning."[8]

Whatever the case, the second Gospel is not meant to be simply an informative collection of facts; the intent of the writer is without a doubt formative, in that he is seeking to persuade the listener to take a position on the person of Jesus, the Son of God, as well as to make a decision regarding their own life. One cannot escape from an encounter with this Gospel unscathed, and the person who reads it in faith is marked in a deep and lasting way. This will also be the manner in which we will approach the Book of Mark through these spiritual exercises. We will apply three questions to this Gospel, which correspond to the three classical stages of the spiritual path, aimed at conversion of the heart and the renewal of life.

---

8. Ibid., 6.

1. Which steps should we take in order to free our-selves from evil and guide our lives firmly in accor-dance with the Father's plan?

2. What choices must we make in order to give full meaning to our lives as followers of Jesus?

3. What are we called to put into practice so that our lives are a source of light and love for others?

We will respond to these three questions in succession as related respectively to the purgative, illuminative, and unitive stages of the spiritual exercises. In light of the Gospel of Mark, we will consider how Jesus comports himself as his life unfolds, how he faces his death, and, finally, how he confronts the future of his mission for us.[9]

In conclusion, let us ask the Spirit for pure eyes in order to see the truth that enlightens and saves. Let us ask him for a pure heart that allows us to be transformed by that truth as we journey along the road of the Son of Man-Son of God, Jesus, and as we encounter him in Mark's narrative:

---

9. The original Italian, *"come si pone di fronte,"* is difficult to translate thoroughly. While in a simple sense it means "to place himself before," at a deeper level it means, "to come face to face with, to confront, to relate to, to consider himself in regard to." This is a key phrase that the author uses throughout the book. — Trans.

Come, O Creator Spirit, visit our minds,
fill with your grace the hearts you created.
O sweet consoler, gift of the most high Father,
living water, fire, love, holy chrism of the soul.
Finger of the hand of God, promised by the Savior,
radiate your seven gifts, inspire in us the word.
Be light to the intellect, a burning flame in our heart;
heal our wounds with the balm of your love.
Protect us from the enemy, bring the gift of peace,
may your invincible guidance preserve us from evil.
Light of eternal wisdom, show us the great mystery
of God the Father and the Son united in one love.
Amen.

CHAPTER 1

Jesus as He Faces His Life

How did Jesus regard himself in relation to his own life? What do his choices ask us to do if we intend to follow him, believe in him, and hope in him?

There are three particular scenes in Mark's account that help us answer these questions:

a) the baptism of Jesus in the Jordan;

b) the temptation in the desert;

c) the description of a typical day of his ministry in Galilee, called the "day of Capernaum."

Baptism in the Jordan

Mark presents the baptism of Jesus thus:

> In those days Jesus came from Nazareth of Galilee and
> was baptized by John in the Jordan. And just as he was
> coming up out of the water, he saw the heavens torn
> apart and the Spirit descending like a dove on him. And
> a voice came from heaven, "You are my Son, the
> Beloved; with you I am well pleased." (Mk 1:9–11)

The scene is introduced by the emphatic formula, typical in Mark, *kai euthys*, which means "and immediately" or "just as." The same expression is found right in the beginning of the account of the temptation of Jesus. It is as if the narrator wishes to emphasize the link between these two events, giving the impression that something decisive is about to take place in them. In the account of the baptism, we are presented with a manifestation of God, a theophany, similar to so many recounted in the Old Testament. Thus, we are told that Jesus has a unique relationship to God and that, through him, a new and decisive phase in the history of salvation is opening up.

The heavens are torn open and the Spirit descends on him. You can hear the invocation of Isaiah echoed, "O that you would tear open the heavens and come down" (Isa 64:1). This is to be fulfilled finally in Jesus, who is both the presence and the voice of God among mankind, the one through whom heaven descends on earth, and opens it to the ultimate horizon, the only one that fully gives meaning to life and to history. The Spirit who hovered over the waters at the first creation (see Gen 1:2) hovers over the waters of the new creation. The voice from heaven reveals the eternal identity of Jesus, "You are my Son, the Beloved; with you I am well pleased" (Mk 1: 11). One recognizes the reference to Psalm 2:7, "He said to me, 'You are my son; today I have begotten you,'" and the sacrifice of Isaac, *the beloved*, in Genesis 22:2. Jesus, the Eternal Son, is the new Isaac offered by the Father for us.

This brings us to clearly understand what is in the consciousness of Jesus at the beginning of his public life. On the one hand, he knows that he is the Son of God, the Beloved. On the other hand, he is aware that he will be handed over in sacrifice for mankind. The joy of the love of the Father unites with the suffering that he will be called to undergo in order to carry out his mission. The Gospel, in short, shows us that anyone who wishes to follow Jesus can certainly count on the consolation of divine love that is offered to us all in him. However, we should also be ready to pay the price of love for our brethren and for their salvation, because the glory of God is fulfilled in this, which is also the good of humanity.

Let us ask ourselves then: Am I willing to trust in the love and faithfulness of God that is revealed in Jesus? Am I

willing to make decisions regarding my life with his example and help? Am I willing to pay the price of love by
following him on his journey of the cross? Do I have faith
in the fact that the Father never abandons his children in
their trials? What resistance do I detect in myself? And
what sins do I confess in order to allow myself to be forgiven and reconciled with the Father so as to be submissive
to his will?

The temptation in the desert

Closely connected to the baptism of Jesus is the scene
of his temptation:

> And the Spirit immediately drove him out into the
> wilderness. He was in the wilderness forty days,
> tempted by Satan; and he was with the wild beasts;
> and the angels waited on him. (Mk 1:12–13)

Matthew and Luke speak of three temptations, mod-
eled after those of Israel in the desert. Thus, they indicate
that the obedience demanded of the Chosen People is fulfilled in Jesus (Mt 4:1–11; Lk 4:1–13). Mark, however, does
not specify which temptation he is dealing with here. In this
way, it seems that Mark is trying to tell us that temptation
was present throughout the entire life of Jesus, and it per-
vaded his mission as beloved Son, come in the flesh, as
indicated at the scene of his baptism (as we have said, the

close relationship between the two scenes is underlined by the repetition of the introductory expression, *kai euthys*, which means "and immediately" or "just as"). The reference to the period of forty days—a number in the Bible that indicates the time span of a generation, but also a privileged time before God—confirms this interpretation.

Moreover, while it is the Spirit who drives Jesus into the desert, it is Satan who comes to tempt him. Throughout Mark's Gospel, this diabolical figure returns in an attempt to oppose God's plan and thwart those who wish to carry it out, beginning with the Eternal Son come in the flesh. Thus, the temptation in the desert is situated in the context of the great battle between the Spirit of God and the Devil, in which the fate of all of us is placed. We can think of temptation as something radical that Adam experienced: trusting in one's self and in the power of the world, instead of trusting in God and in one's own weakness. Saint Augustine expressed this choice well, "Love of one's self to the point of forgetting God, or love of God to the point of forgetting one's self."[1]

Jesus perceives the seduction of the other side, which seemed to be more incisive. On the one hand, he feels the appeal of a political and worldly messianism, which was so

---

1. Saint Augustine, *De Civitate Dei*, XIV, 28.

widespread among his own people with whom he shared the pain of oppression. On the other hand, he is faced with the messianism of prophetic obedience, which he came to know through conversation with his Father, especially while reading of the Suffering Servant and the prophets in Scripture. He must choose between trusting in the judgment of God and the logic of the Prince of this world. The Nazarene said "no" to the propositions of his time and of all times: pleasure, possession, power. He does not seek popular approval, nor does he give in to the attraction of immediate results. Jesus chooses the Father. In an act of complete freedom, he prefers obedience to God and personal self-denial, to obedience to self and denial of the Father. He entrusts himself with unwavering certainty to the Father and he intends to fulfill God's plan regardless of how dark and painful it may appear. During his temptation, Jesus demonstrates that he is free from himself, free for his Father and for others, free through the freedom of love. In Jesus, the unconditionally obedient Servant, the stairway of prophetic obedience reaches its highest point. Jesus testifies that if we rely on God during temptation, the Father will not abandon us. Instead, he will help open our eyes to the truth about ourselves and the world, which Satan wishes to obscure. Unconditional trust in God is the only true freedom from evil, and it is the only way to fulfill God's plan in history!

Am I ready to do this without any excuses? Do I recognize that he alone is the Lord who heals us? And that his word has the power to make us whole?

The day of Capernaum

The fundamental option of loving his Father and other people thus inspired the choices Jesus made in regard to his life and his mission. How did he act upon them? Mark gives us a meaningful answer in his narration of a typical day of the Galilean prophet's ministry, and by describing the activities of Jesus through his process of alternating between events of revelation and invitations to discretion and silence. This has been called the messianic secret. The day of Capernaum is presented as follows:

> They went to Capernaum; and when the sabbath came, he entered the synagogue and taught. They were astounded at his teaching, for he taught them as one having authority, and not as the scribes. Just then there was in their synagogue a man with an unclean spirit, and he cried out, "What have you to do with us, Jesus of Nazareth? Have you come to destroy us? I know who you are, the Holy One of God." But Jesus rebuked him, saying, "Be silent, and come out of him!" And the unclean spirit, convulsing him and crying with a loud voice, came out of him. They were all amazed, and they kept on asking one another, "What

is this? A new teaching—with authority! He commands even the unclean spirits, and they obey him." At once his fame began to spread throughout the surrounding region of Galilee.

As soon as they left the synagogue, they entered the house of Simon and Andrew, with James and John. Now Simon's mother-in-law was in bed with a fever, and they told him about her at once. He came and took her by the hand and lifted her up. Then the fever left her, and she began to serve them. That evening, at sundown, they brought to him all who were sick or possessed with demons. And the whole city was gathered around the door. And he cured many who were sick with various diseases, and cast out many demons; and he would not permit the demons to speak, because they knew him.

In the morning, while it was still very dark, he got up and went out to a deserted place, and there he prayed. And Simon and his companions hunted for him. When they found him, they said to him, "Everyone is searching for you." He answered, "Let us go on to the neighboring towns, so that I may proclaim the message there also; for that is what I came out to do." And he went throughout Galilee, proclaiming the message in their synagogues and casting out demons.

A leper came to him begging him, and kneeling he said to him, "If you choose, you can make me clean." Moved with pity, Jesus stretched out his hand and touched him, and said to him, "I do choose. Be made clean!" Immediately the leprosy left him, and he was made clean. After sternly warning him he sent him away at once, saying to him, "See that you say nothing to anyone; but go, show yourself to the priest, and offer for your cleansing what Moses commanded, as a testimony to them." But he went out and began to proclaim it freely, and to spread the word, so that Jesus could no longer go into a town openly, but stayed out in the country; and people came to him from every quarter. (Mk 1:21–45)

First of all, we should note the geographical and social context of the scene. It takes place at the city gate, which was a place of commerce and trade, as well as a gathering place to resolve disputes. It also occurs in the synagogue, in the house of Simon, and finally in a deserted place. Jesus does not retreat from life's events; rather, he engages the world in its multiplicity of places and dealings. One could say that he is anything but a solitary hermit, someone who would flee from human relationships; on the contrary, he lives out his identity and mission everywhere and reaches people where they are and where they live their lives. The activities of Jesus are basically four.

The first is *teaching*. When Jesus taught, he aroused awe, for "he taught them as one having authority, and not as the scribes" (1:22). Jesus teaches authoritatively and he does not repeat what is already known, but he presents the newness of the kingdom of God that comes in the very person who proclaims it. It is, in fact, "a new teaching" (1:27). Jesus is the first evangelizer, and he witnesses by his own way of acting that the proclamation of the truth that liberates and saves must be placed before everything.

The second activity of the Galilean prophet is *freedom* from evil. There is no trace of naiveté in the Nazarene; he does not close his eyes to this tragic aspect in human history. There is an ongoing struggle against the Evil One who wishes to separate people from God, from each other, and from themselves. This struggle must be confronted honestly by aiming directly at freedom from the evil and sin carried in people's hearts. Jesus tells us that Satan is at work, and the danger he poses should never be underestimated. New life cannot begin without first being freed from the snares of the Prince of this world. This is the tragic reality of the redemptive work of the Son of God and of accepting his action in faith. It is essential to fight, resist, and overcome the Adversary with the strength that the Son of God came to bring to us. The temptation to hide this aspect from one's self and underestimate the devastating power of sin, or to take shortcuts by seeking quick miracles, is always present in the human heart. It is difficult for everyone to accept hardship as a result of the decisions we must make and the things we must cease doing. But through his actions, Jesus unmasks every excuse and places before us the necessary choice.

The third activity that takes place in the day of the Nazarene is that of *healings*. These are a result of freedom from evil, and, in a certain sense, they represent a positive aspect of the work of the Messiah. The miracles that Jesus performs are a sign of the kingdom of God. At the same time, they presuppose and produce faith. Miracles presuppose faith because the power of God does not impose itself aggressively on people; rather, it enters in when one opens him or herself up through faith. Miracles produce faith because the powerful sign of the coming of salvation brings forth trust and the action of grace. Through his action, the Nazarene instructs us to continually measure ourselves against the impossible possibility of God. We are to reason not with evidence, but with the unknown and the incalculability that the mercy of God is capable of rousing for love of humanity. Jesus is aware that the miracles he accomplishes could be interpreted ambiguously; that is, his signs could attract people more to the benefits they hoped to obtain instead of to the challenging discipleship of love demanded by his word and life. This is why he does not allow the deceiving demons to talk (see Mk 1:34), and he retreats to solitude, going off early in the morning into the desert. Just so, he invites us to always first seek interior healing.

And it is there, in solitude, that Jesus lives the fourth fundamental activity of his day: *prayer*. The Italian text says that Jesus "was praying" (Mk 1:35). The use of the imperfect verb tense indicates a sense of continuity.[2] Thus, prayer for Jesus is uninterrupted, which is more visible in some strong moments, yet always alive and profound. The substance of his prayer will be revealed only at the moment of Gethsemane—when he pours out everything in his relationship with his Father. Jesus puts his faith in his Father, he confides in him, he trusts him.[3] He does this despite what is humanly incomprehensible and brutal. Thus, prayer marks the entire journey and mission of Jesus (see Mk 1:45; 6:46). One cannot live in obedience to the Father without a continual immersion in loving dialogue with him and without continuously entrusting oneself anew into the Father's hands!

If in relation to God the Father, the Nazarene seeks to experience continuous prayer and moments of retreat in deserted places, in relation to people, he shuns all exploitation of the miraculous and he desires in every way to avoid

---

2. The Italian biblical source from which the author is quoting uses the word *pregava*, meaning "he was praying." This is the imperfect Italian past tense which indicates, as the author says, an ongoing action in the past. The biblical text we quoted utilizes the simple past tense (preterite), "he prayed." —Trans.

3. In the original Italian text, "Lui si affida, in Lui confida, di Lui si fida," the author plays on three words with the same Latin root, *fides*, meaning "faith or trust." —Trans.

any possible misunderstanding of his mission. Thus, he seeks to bring everything into the divine plan. And seeing this in relation to his life and work, we find the summons to discretion, the order to be silent (given, for example, to the man with an unclean spirit in the synagogue or to the healed leper), which has been called the messianic secret. It helps us to properly understand the effectiveness of our own prayer, which sometimes may not seem to be evidently or immediately valuable.

In the first place, the messianic secret is a literary device, with which the evangelist wishes to gradually lead the hearers of his Gospel to recognize and profess the messianic role of Jesus; that is, that he was the Son of God who came into this world to save us. In this sense, the catechumen is led by the hand down the pathway of initiation into the mystery of Christ. Nonetheless, it is not unfounded to conclude that the logic of his revelation-concealment is an intentional choice of the Nazarene himself. In this, Jesus is seeking not to enchant people with signs of power or amazing revelations, but rather to introduce them to an encounter of faith and love with him and with his heavenly Father, while completely respecting their freedom. Thus, Jesus prepares his followers to recognize him as the Son of God during his hour of abandonment and defeat on the cross, not in wonder and power. And this is how he instructs them to the faith he lived during the darkness of

Good Friday, as well as the blinding light of Easter. The Son of God (a title repeated seven times in Mark) is the Servant. In humiliation and death he reveals his eternal identity and his mission throughout time.

Finally, in the messianic secret, the faith of Jesus emerges inasmuch as he is a man. On the night of his earthly life, he advances toward the light of the final victory while trusting in the Father, whose loyalty he never doubts, even at the hour of his abandonment (see Mk 15:36; Lk 23:42). If the Master does so, how should the disciples behave? Will they not be called to go forth into the darkness of faith toward the light of the vision, supported only by faith in the promises of God and by the strengthening power of prayer?

Let us now ask ourselves how we pray? Do we abandon ourselves to God, to his will and his timing, or do we place deadlines and conditions? Do we immediately want the light or do we accept going forward in the dark, illuminated only by the word of God, like the *servus lampadarius*[4] of our ancient forbears who illuminated each section of

---

4. In the ancient Roman world, the *servus lampadarius* (torch-bearing servant) was the servant whose job it was to precede his master with a torch to light the way in the night. The light did not illuminate the entire pathway, but only that portion along which they were traveling. — Trans.

the road just a little at a time, allowing only enough light to take the next step?

Therefore, in regard to his life and his mission, Jesus is presented by Mark as a man who lives his nature both as beloved Son of the heavenly Father and as Isaac, offered up in sacrifice by the same loving Father for us all. Glory and cross unite from the beginning of his awareness of his identity and mission. From his relationship of Son to the Father, Jesus draws light and strength in order to face his destiny on the cross in total freedom from self, out of love of God and humanity. His unconditional "yes" is put to the test by the hostility of the Adversary, but the Spirit does not abandon Jesus, and Jesus does not abandon the Father. The way of truth is tried and ends up victorious. The Galilean Prophet's life is a gift of self and divine life to mankind marked by teaching, deliverance from evil, healings, and prayer rooted in the heart of the Father. In the ordinariness of life's relationships, Jesus offers the news of salvation for our life that comes from above. He does so reservedly and with discretion in order to avoid any misunderstandings and to lead his disciples to accept the logic of the cross in which glory both reveals and gives itself.

To Jesus, as we see him in relation to his own life and mission, we turn in prayer as pilgrims in this night of faith. Let us, who are called to follow him in his choices, decide for ourselves before the Father as Jesus decided, with the help that only he can give. Let us do so with the words of one of the great converts of the twentieth century, Giovanni Papini,[5] while we question ourselves about our own life choices and the faithfulness with which we intend to follow the Lord:

> We need you alone and no one else. You alone, who love us, can feel for all of us who suffer the compassion that each of us feels for himself. Only you can feel how immeasurably great is the need for you in this world, in this hour of the world. . . . Everyone needs you, even those who do not know it, and those who do not know it need you so much more than those who do know it. . . . Those who seek beauty in the world seek you without realizing it—you who are full and perfect beauty; those who seek truth in their thoughts, desire, without meaning to, you, who are the only truth worthy of being known, and those who struggle for peace seek you, the only peace where they can rest their most restless hearts. They call you without knowing that they are calling you, and their cry is inexpressibly more painful than ours. . . . But we, the last ones, wait for you. We will wait for you

---

5. Giovanni Papini (1881–1956) was a controversial journalist, poet, novelist, and critic of Christianity who converted to Catholicism in 1920 and authored the internationally acclaimed novel *Storia di Cristo*. — Ed.

every day, in spite of our unworthiness and every adversity. And all the love that we can press from our devastated hearts will be for you, the Crucified One, who was tortured out of love for us, and who now torments us with all the power of your relentless love.[6]

---

6. The concluding prayer in Giovanni Papini, *Storia di Cristo* (Firenze: Vallecchi, 1922).

CHAPTER 2

Jesus as He Faces His Death

It is rightly said that death is the touchstone of all humanity and of the fundamental choices that characterize each person. After having looked at how Jesus comports himself as his life unfolds, we now ask ourselves how he faces his own death. We are now at the heart of the illuminative stage of the spiritual exercises, because only those who give meaning to death can also give value and meaning to life. Mark helps us grasp the way Jesus sees and undergoes his death:

a) in his repeated pronouncements of his passion;

b) in the scene of Gethsemane; and

c) in his death on the cross.

The pronouncements of his passion

Halfway through his narrative, in the eighth chapter, Mark introduces a passage that marks a turning point in the life of the protagonist, Jesus. It is the first pronouncement of his passion. To put it into context, Jesus is asking his disciples what they understood about him. It is as if he wants to be clear with them, openly presenting his destiny on the cross as the most appropriate way to get to the heart of his mystery. Mark narrates:

> Jesus went on with his disciples to the village of Caesarea Philippi; and on the way he asked his disciples, "Who do people say that I am?" And they answered him, "John the Baptist; and others, Elijah; and still others, one of the prophets." He asked them, "But who do you say that I am?" Peter answered him, "You are the Messiah." And he sternly ordered them not to tell anyone about him.
>
> Then he began to teach them that the Son of Man must undergo great suffering, and be rejected by the elders, the chief priests, and the scribes, and be killed, and after three days rise again. He said all this quite openly. And Peter took him aside and began to rebuke him. But turning and looking at his disciples, he rebuked Peter and said, "Get behind me, Satan! For you are setting your mind not on divine things but on human things." (Mk 8:27–33)

His question, "But who do you say that I am?" places the foundation of faith in Jesus. Therefore, it is put forward at the center not only of the account of the Master's life, but also at the center of the belief of the disciple who responds to the question. Anyone who wishes to deal with Jesus seriously cannot escape this question about his identity. It should be noted, at the outset, that it is Jesus who asks the question. At the moment he becomes the object of the question, it is still he who questions. It is as if the evangelist wants to make clear that Christ's reflection must reverse the usual order of the search. The object must become the subject. The stance must change so that the "relationship to him must not be one of questioning, but of being questioned; must not be one of demanding an answer, but of giving an answer."[1] The heart of the reflection and of the Christian faith is not an object, a doctrine, or a formula; rather, it is the living Jesus who provokes and disturbs. Jesus will not be limited by notions and conceptions that people would attempt to apply to him. The catechumen must realize that the encounter with Christ

---

1. Jürgen Moltmann, *The Crucified God: The Cross of Christ as the Foundation and Criticism of Christian Theology* (New York: Harper & Row, Publishers, 1974), 103.

calls for total openness toward the surprises at the advent
of God, awe before the One who comes. Giovanni Papini
describes this thought well: "We, the last ones, wait for
you. We will wait for you every day . . . the Crucified One,
who was tortured out of love for us, and who now torments us with all the power of your relentless love."[2] The
Christian should live out, at the center of his very being,
the mystery of Christ's coming!

According to the account, Jesus raises two questions.
The first deals with what people say about him, while the
second challenges the disciples directly, "Who do you say
that I am?" Jesus does not seem contented with what others say about him; rather, he wants an answer directly
from the disciples, not one based on hearsay. Jesus wants
the word to come alive; he forces them to reveal their own
refusal or acceptance. Whatever we do with Jesus cannot
be harmless or marginal. To seek his face means to allow
oneself to become disturbed, to choose sides, to set aside
one's reassuring certainties in their uncompromising positions. Faith is involvement, passion, mind, and heart
beating together in an attempt to answer the question of
Christ, which engages one's life.

Peter responds to the question of the Nazarene, "You
are the Messiah" (8:29). What Peter really means will

2. Papini, *Storia di Cristo*, 549.

become apparent in what happens next: Jesus begins to teach that the Son of Man must suffer many things, be rejected by the elders, chief priests and scribes, be killed, and rise again after three days; Peter is shocked, and he takes Jesus aside and begins to rebuke him. In this way, he appears like the catechumen who states all his human objections to the logic of the cross! The reaction of Jesus is clear, "Get behind me, Satan! For you are setting your mind not on divine things but on human things" (8:33). We can surmise that whatever Peter had hoped for, it was not a suffering Messiah and an agonizing Christ. Perhaps he, too, had dreamed of the coming of a Messiah who, according to the hopes and expectations of his time, would deliver Israel and end their current humiliation in fulfillment of the promises of the God of their fathers.

Against this expectation, Jesus presents a scandalous picture of himself. After having asked the question about his identity, he announces the story of his passion for the first time. He speaks of himself as the Son of Man, a title used fourteen times in Mark. This title refers in the majority of times to Jesus as a man of sorrows or a rejected prophet. As the Son of Man, Jesus says that he himself must suffer. The Greek verb *déi* means "must" and refers then to the plan that the Father conceives, while freely relating to the events of human freedom, the plan which the Son adhered to out of loving obedience. By connecting this perspective to the question of his identity, the Nazarene seems to want to indicate the place where one can recognize his face—precisely on the way of the cross. It is almost as if the mystery of glory is revealed *sub contraria species* (in its opposite) in the darkness of suffering, condemnation, and death on Good Friday. Peter's expectation is contradicted and broken, and with it all those expectations that, throughout the ages, have been projected on the Christ. Jesus is not the response to our expectations; rather, he subverts our questions. He disrupts all human ways of speaking about him, all attempts to limit him within our own conceptions and notions. Too often we would want to nail Christ to the cross of our expectations, rather than nailing our expectations on the cross of Christ!

Jesus overturns this way of thinking. Those who reason humanly cannot reach the heart of his mystery, rather only those who obediently listen to God. Nor can someone proclaim the Gospel who wants to satisfy the preferences of their listeners, but only the one who has the courage to challenge and change them. In other words, as Jürgen Moltmann inferred: "If we want to know who God is, we must kneel at the foot of the cross."[3] And together, we must open ourselves to the impossible possibility that

---

3. See Moltmann, *The Crucified God*, 55.

was disclosed at Easter. Those who look elsewhere do not reason like God, but as human beings, even like Peter who properly acknowledged with his words that Jesus is the Christ, the Messiah. "If any want to become my followers, let them deny themselves and take up their cross and follow me. For those who want to save their life will lose it, and those who lose their life for my sake, and for the sake of the gospel, will save it" (Mk 8:34–35). We must follow the Master not expecting to go ahead of him, guiding him along the way that *we* would wish. We must deny ourselves; that is, remove from ourselves our ego, and put the Lord in its place! While confronting the reality of his final destiny, Jesus turns the logic of human expectations upside down. In this, we understand that Jesus sees death completely in the realm of obedience to God's plan. And this is what the Master asks also of his disciples. The radical question is imposed, then, on each of us—hearers of and participants in Mark's Gospel: Will I allow myself to be turned upside down by Christ? Am I ready to allow myself to be brought where I would not want, dream, or hope to go, but where God wants and knows is good for me, even unto death?

The prophecy of the passion returns two more times:

> They left from there and began a journey through Galilee, but he did not wish anyone to know about it. He was teaching his disciples and telling them, "The

> Son of Man is to be handed over to men and they will
> kill him, and three days after his death he will rise."
> But they did not understand the saying, and they were
> afraid to question him. (Mk 9:30–32 NABRE)

> They were on the road, going up to Jerusalem, and
> Jesus was walking ahead of them; they were amazed,
> and those who followed were afraid. He took the
> twelve aside again and began to tell them what was to
> happen to him, saying, "See, we are going up to
> Jerusalem, and the Son of Man will be handed over to
> the chief priests and the scribes, and they will con-
> demn him to death; then they will hand him over to
> the Gentiles; they will mock him, and spit upon him,
> and flog him, and kill him; and after three days he will
> rise again." (Mk 10:32–34)

There are three striking elements in these verses. Jesus
speaks of his *via dolorosa* at the heart of his ministry, while
walking along with his disciples. The perspective of the
cross, then, arises on the road of all who set out to follow
him, and it envelops the ordinariness of their works and
life. No one who wants to follow Jesus can get away from
it. The reaction of the disciples is extremely human. They
do not understand; they are defensive, afraid, and trou-
bled. They instinctively reject what appears to be anything
but desirable and attractive.

Christ's threefold prophesying of his passion demonstrates just how central it was in his awareness of his

identity. Additionally, it shows just how much he wanted to communicate to his disciples that following him inevitably means embracing the same agonizing destiny. Even if the three prophecies of the passion were, as some exegetes would have it, *vaticinia ex eventu*, that is, a foretelling after the event has already taken place, it is clear that the intent of the evangelist is to familiarize the catechumen with the centrality and inescapability of the Way of the Cross. Mark does not accommodate the Gospel to the potential preferences of those who hear it; rather, he focuses strongly on its demand of love, for which Jesus gave himself up and against which one measures the authenticity of his or her being a follower of the Son of Man. At the foundation of this demanding calling, there must be the will of Jesus to acknowledge his own destiny by recognizing in himself the figure of the persecuted righteous one presented in the psalms (see Ps 22; 28; 43; 54) and in the songs of the Suffering Servant of Isaiah (see Is 42:1–9; 49:1–12; 50:4-9; 52:13–53:12), open and willing to pay the price of love, but also confident in the faithfulness and final victory of God.

The prayer in the Garden of Olives

The choice to obey the loving plan of the Father in complete freedom until the end is confirmed by Jesus in the dramatic hour that preceded his passion and death. It is the prayer in the Garden of Olives, Gethsemane:

> They went to a place called Gethsemane; and he said to his disciples, "Sit here while I pray." He took with him Peter and James and John, and began to be distressed and agitated. And he said to them, "I am deeply grieved, even to death; remain here, and keep awake." And going a little farther, he threw himself on the ground and prayed that, if it were possible, the hour might pass from him. He said, "Abba, Father, for you all things are possible; remove this cup from me; yet, not what I want, but what you want." He came and found them sleeping; and he said to Peter, "Simon, are you asleep? Could you not keep awake one hour? Keep awake and pray that you may not come into the time of trial; the spirit indeed is willing, but the flesh is weak." And again he went away and prayed, saying the same words. And once more he came and found them sleeping, for their eyes were very heavy; and they did not know what to say to him. He came a third time and said to them, "Are you still sleeping and taking your rest? Enough! The hour has come; the Son of Man is betrayed into the hands of sinners. Get up, let us be going. See, my betrayer is at hand." (Mk 14:32–42)

The agony of Gethsemane clearly reveals how Jesus positions himself in regard to his death. He is at the end of his journey, at the moment in which the extreme consequence of his choice of love for the Father and for mankind is before him. He is so affected by the temptation to escape his suffering that he sweats blood (see Lk 22:44). Like Matthew, Mark speaks of the distress Jesus experiences (see Mk 14:33; Mt 26:37), his grief (see Mk 14:34; Mt 26:38), his fear (Mk 14:33). Jesus seems to feel an immense need for close friendship: "Remain here and keep awake" (Mk 14:34; Mt 26:38). But he is left alone, terribly alone, faced with his future, as probably occurs in everyone's fundamental choices: "Simon, are you asleep? Could you not keep awake one hour?" (Mk 14:37). "So, could you not stay awake with me one hour?" (Mt 26:40). The radical choice stands before him in the most violent way: to save his life or to lose it, to choose between his will and the will of his Father. "Abba, Father, for you all things are possible; remove this cup from me" (Mk 14:36). In the moment in which he affirms his "yes" in accordance with his radical freedom, Jesus clings totally to his Father and calls him with the name of trust and tenderness, "Abba! . . . not what I want, but what you want" (Mk 14:36). It is significant that this is the only time in the Gospels that the Aramaic is conserved in the familiar form while invoking his Father: "Abba," which means "Papa" or "Dad"!

The "yes" of Jesus is the fruit of love without reservation; his is the freedom of love! In the final hour, he still chooses to give of himself, and he places himself back into the hands of his Father with an infinite trust. He experiences his freedom as liberation: liberation of himself for his Father and for others. It is the freedom of those who find their life by losing it (see Mk 8:35), the capacity of risking everything for love, the audacity of those who give everything. Thus, the fundamental aspiration of Jesus emerges, the choice on which he bases every choice, the vocation of his life. It is what the author of the Letter to the Hebrews faithfully translated from the words of Psalm 40:9, "See, I have come to do your will" (Heb 10:9). In the profound plan of liberty—the radical desire that gives meaning and unity to everything in life—Jesus presents himself as a man free for love, totally aimed toward the Father and others. He testifies that no one is so free as the one who is free from their own freedom because of greater love. Free of himself, Jesus exists for the Father and for others; this is his fundamental choice, the one that makes him truly a free man. The basis of his life is to exist for the kingdom that comes. This is his vocation, and it makes of his entire existence a liturgy to God. For this reason, he asks the disciple: Are you free from yourself? Free to obey God? Are you free to obey God alone? Are you free to love to the point of the greatest gift? Do you know how to recognize that next to each disciple is the Master, and so as a Christian you are never alone, in joy and in sorrow, in peace and in trials, in life as in death?

His death on the cross

Jesus lives his death in light of the choices he made. Mark's essential account of the cross offers sufficient information to understand this:

> Then they brought Jesus to the place called Golgotha (which means the place of a skull). And they offered him wine mixed with myrrh; but he did not take it. And they crucified him, and divided his clothes among them, casting lots to decide what each should take.
>
> It was nine o'clock in the morning when they crucified him. The inscription of the charge against him read, "The King of the Jews." And with him they crucified two bandits, one on his right and one on his left. Those who passed by derided him, shaking their heads and saying, "Aha! You who would destroy the temple and build it in three days, save yourself, and come down from the cross!" In the same way the chief priests, along with the scribes, were also mocking him among themselves and saying, "He saved others; he cannot save himself. Let the Messiah, the King of Israel, come down from the cross now, so that we may see and believe." Those who were crucified with him also taunted him.
>
> When it was noon, darkness came over the whole land until three in the afternoon. At three o'clock Jesus cried out with a loud voice, "Eloi, Eloi, lema sabachthani?" which means, "My God, my God, why have you forsaken me?" When some of the bystanders heard it, they said, "Listen, he is calling for Elijah."

> And someone ran, filled a sponge with sour wine, put it on a stick, and gave it to him to drink, saying, "Wait, let us see whether Elijah will come to take him down." Then Jesus gave a loud cry and breathed his last. And the curtain of the temple was torn in two, from top to bottom. Now when the centurion, who stood facing him, saw that in this way he breathed his last, he said, "Truly this man was God's Son!" (Mk 15:22–39)

The carrying out of the unjust condemnation is presented by Mark with strong images. These highlight the contrast between the human betrayal of Jesus and his divine deliverance. On the one hand, there are the taunts of the passersby—the chief priests, the scribes, and even those of his close companions (15:29–32). Additionally, the darkness that came over the land seems to say that even the sky forgot about this man, abandoned by all. On the other hand, the tearing of the curtain of the veil of the temple (15:38) and the profession of the centurion who recognizes him as the Son of God upon seeing Jesus die in this way (15:39) allude to a very different message. What was inaccessible becomes accessible because the death of that crucified One is the death of the Son of God who conquers death! In reality, the Son delivered himself to his God and Father out of love for us and in our place, with all the weight of that painful offering. In handing himself over, the crucified One took upon himself the world's burden of pain and sin. He entered directly into the exile of sinners from God in order to assume this exile in his deliverance and in the paschal reconciliation. Paul spells it out clearly: "Christ redeemed us from the curse of the law by becoming a curse for us—for it is written, 'Cursed is everyone who hangs on a tree'—in order that in Christ Jesus the blessing of Abraham might come to the Gentiles, so that we might receive the promise of the Spirit through faith" (Gal 3:13–14).

In this light, the cry of the dying Jesus appears as a sign of the most profound sorrow and exile that the Son came to assume in order to enter into the deepest suffering of the world and reconcile it with the Father: "My God, my God, why have you forsaken me?" (Mk 15:34; see Mt 27:46). Jesus is the abandoned One, but he does not despair; on the contrary, he totally abandons himself into the hands of his Father, as the evangelist Luke expresses by quoting Psalm 31:5, "Father, into your hands I commend my spirit" (Lk 23:46).

The Father remains the constant reference in the life and death of Jesus, as the entire Gospel of Mark emphasizes. It is understandable, then, how the Son's handing over of himself corresponds to the deliverance of the Father, indicated by what is called the method of the *divine passive*. "The Son of Man is to be handed over to men and they will kill him" (Mk 9:31 NABRE; see Mk 10:33, 45; Mk 14:41; Mt 26:45–46).[4] It is not men who betray him, even though he is betrayed by their hands. Nor will it only be Jesus who hands himself over, since the verb is in the passive voice. The one who will hand him over will be God, his Father. Paul reflects on this message, "He who did not withhold his own Son, but gave him up for all of us, will he not with him also give us everything else?" (Rom 8:32). In giving up his own Son for us, the Father reveals the depth of his love for mankind: "In this is love, not that we loved God but that he loved us and sent his Son to be the atoning sacrifice for our sins" (1 Jn 4:10; see Rom 5:6–11).

As the meditation inspired by the first Christian community clearly affirms, the cross reveals that God, the Father, is love! (see 1 Jn 4:8–16). The suffering of the Father, closely analogous to that of Abraham who offered his only begotten son, Isaac (see Gen 22:12; Jn 3:16; 1 Jn 4:9), is nothing else than the other aspect of his infinite love: "The Father, God of the universe, patient and merciful, feels

---

4. The Italian Bible that the author quotes from uses the word *consegna*, which is translated "betrayed" in *The New Revised Standard Version*, the biblical text from which we have quoted. It also means, "offered, delivered, given up, or handed over" and has been translated according to its various meanings here and throughout the book. —Trans.

pain in a certain sense. . . . The Father himself is not without pain! If someone beseeches him, he is seized with mercy and compassion; he suffers through love; he has feelings that he could not have according to his sublime nature. Regarding us, he feels human pain" (Origen, *Homily on Ezekiel,* 6.6).

The Son's handing over of himself and the Father's delivering him, therefore, are signs of supreme love that changes history: "No one has greater love than this, to lay down one's life for one's friends" (Jn 15:13). The suffering of the Son is matched by the suffering of the Father. God suffers on the cross as the Father who offers, as the Son who offers himself, while the Spirit is the love that emanates from their suffering love. The Christian God is not outside the suffering of the world, as a spectator seated on the throne of absolute perfection, incapable of suffering. Rather, God takes on suffering and lives it most intensely, actively, as a gift and an offering from which springs the new life of the world. Since Good Friday, we know that the Christian God shares the human story of suffering. He is present in it, and he suffers with humanity to teach us the immense value of suffering offered out of love. He does not remain a hidden counterpart to whom the suffering and desolate cry out in hope of being lifted up; rather, he is "in a more profound sense, the human God, who cries out in man and with him, and intervenes on his behalf with his cross when man falls silent in his torments."[5] It is God who gives meaning to suffering in the world, because he has assumed it to the extent of making suffering his own: this meaning is love.

The abandonment of the Son by the Father reveals the greatness of their love for humanity, the profundity of their unity in divine being, and their desire for the salvation of the world. The pain of separation points to the abyss of communion—greater than any distance—that shall be revealed in the final victory over death on Easter. The exile of the Son in the world, his becoming *cursed* in the land of those cursed by God, has in his Father's plan the purpose that sinners, having been forgiven and redeemed, can enter together with the Son into the joy of paschal reconciliation. "For our sake he made him to be sin who knew no sin, so that in him we might become the righteousness of God" (2 Cor 5:21; see Rom 8:3). In the face of such rending of so unfathomable a unity, we can understand the profession of the centurion, which took place at the peak of the catechumenal journey where Mark has led his hearers: "Truly this man was God's Son" (Mk 15:39).

---

5. Jürgen Moltmann, *Il Dio crocifisso. Il problema moderno di Dio e la storia trinitaria di Dio* (Conciliun, 1972), 1085.

The manner in which Jesus faces his death is, then, the message of life and hope for all who shall believe in him. Death can also be for them a way of loving surrender; what is impossible with human strength becomes possible with Jesus Crucified as our companion. It is this *possible-impossible* love that the Son of God, who became man for us, has revealed and given to us. We are all called to this.

A positive example of such love is demonstrated by the exemplary teaching and actions of the Pakistani Minister for Minorities Affairs, Shahbaz Bhatti. This Christian politician had received various threats from extremists. Nevertheless, their intimidation did not cause him to discontinue his commitment to the defense of minorities. He was eventually assassinated by gunfire in Islamabad, the capital of Pakistan, on March 2, 2011. What follows he recorded in his testament, clearly foreseeing the possibility of his sacrifice in the example of and with the help of Jesus:

> My name is Shahbaz Bhatti. I was born into a Catholic family. My father, a retired teacher, and my mother, a housewife, raised me according to Christian values and biblical teachings that influenced my childhood. As a boy, I used to go to church where I found profound inspiration in the teachings, sacrifice, and crucifixion of Jesus. It was the love of Jesus that led me to offer my service to the Church. I was shocked by the appalling conditions in which Pakistani

Christians were living. I remember listening to a Good Friday sermon when I was only thirteen years old. It was about the sacrifice of Jesus for our redemption and the salvation of the world. And I thought to respond to his love by loving our brothers and sisters and by placing myself at the service of Christians, especially the poor, needy, and persecuted who live in this Muslim country. It was eventually asked of me to cease my battle, but I always refused, even at the risk of my own life. My answer was always the same. I do not want popularity or positions of power. I only want a place at the feet of Jesus. I want my life, character, and actions to speak for me and say that I am a follower of Jesus Christ. This desire is so strong in me that I would consider myself privileged should Jesus accept the sacrifice of my life in this combative effort of mine to help the needy, poor, and persecuted Christians of Pakistan. I want to live for Christ; I want to die for him. I do not feel any fear in this country. Many times the extremists have wanted to kill me or imprison me; they have threatened me, harassed me, and even terrorized my family. I say that as long as I live and until my last breath, I will continue to serve Jesus and this poor suffering humanity, the Christians, the needy, the poor. I see that Christians throughout the world have reached out to Muslims affected by the tragic earthquake of 2005; we built bridges of solidarity, love, understanding, cooperation, and tolerance between the two religions. If these efforts continue, I am confident that we will succeed in winning the hearts and minds of the extremists. This will bring a positive change. People will no longer hate one another or kill in the name of religion; rather, they will love each other, they will bring harmony, they will cultivate peace and understanding in this region. I think the needy, the poor, and the orphans, whatever their religion, should be regarded first and foremost as human beings. I think that these people are part of my body in Christ and that they are the persecuted and needy part of the body of Christ. If we carry out this mission, then we will have earned a place at the feet of Jesus, and I will be able to look at him with no shame.[6]

6. Cf. F. Milano, *Morte di un blasfemo: Shahbaz Bhatti, un politico martire in Pakistan* (Cinisello Balsamo: Edizioni San Paolo, 2012).

CHAPTER 3

Jesus as He Faces
the Future of His Mission

A s is the case of every life fully lived, the life and mis-sion of Jesus are inseparable from the future that opens up before him. His is a future that embraces every-one of every age who will be reached by his good news of love through the gift of new life in his Spirit. How does the Nazarene place himself in this scenario? And how shall those who believe in him and choose to follow him con-sider themselves and their journey as people of God in light of his resurrection, in time and for eternity? Mark responds to these questions through his account of the empty tomb, which is a sort of unfinished storyline that seems to break off at its most beautiful point. But in reality, it constitutes an authentic summary of the entire Gospel, and it is an appealing call to faith in the Risen Lord and to following him.

The empty tomb

> When the sabbath was over, Mary Magdalene, and Mary the mother of James, and Salome bought spices, so that they might go and anoint him. And very early on the first day of the week, when the sun had risen, they went to the tomb. They had been saying to one another, "Who will roll away the stone for us from the entrance to the tomb?" When they looked up, they saw that the stone, which was very large, had already been rolled back. As they entered the tomb, they saw a young man, dressed in a white robe, sitting on the right side; and they were alarmed. But he said to them, "Do not be alarmed; you are looking for Jesus of Nazareth, who was crucified. He has been raised; he is not here. Look, there is the place they laid him. But go, tell his disciples and Peter that he is going ahead of you to Galilee; there you will see him, just as he told you." So they went out and fled from the tomb, for terror and amazement had seized them; and they said nothing to anyone, for they were afraid. (Mk 16:1–8)

Most likely the original account of Mark ended here at chapter sixteen, verse eight. At first glance, this is problematic and paradoxical, as we would be confronted with an open-ended story. Verses nine through twenty that follow are canonical, because they are included in the canon of texts recognized as inspired by the faith of the Church; yet, they are not found in the most ancient manuscripts, for example in the *Codex Sinaiticus* and the *Codex Vaticanus*. Also, they have a style that differs from the rest of the account. In fact, the evangelist may have intentionally wanted to leave his narrative open-ended. He may have intended for his Gospel to be understood as continuing in the lives of its hearers. After having been accompanied to their baptism, whatever the catechumens do after their rebirth would become a *sequentia sancti Evangelii*, a continuation of the holy Gospel, a story narrated in people of every place, time, and situation.

The continuous movement in the structural narrative of these eight verses is striking. It is a metaphor of the Christian journey of life. The women go to the tomb and enter because the stone had been rolled back; then they go out and flee full of fear and amazement. Just as in Mark's Gospel Jesus often requires the so-called messianic secret, the women are silent and taken aback by the striking event they just witnessed. When one encounters the Lord and feels mandated by him to announce it, the overwhelming nature of what was just experienced, when confronted by words, seems to lead to a silence overflowing with life, newness, and meaning. Here, Mark shows that he is an expert teacher of catechumens: he enkindles desire and communicates enough light to satisfy it; he leaves open the way for the Lord to accomplish his work in each person, while allowing each person the freedom and discretion to accept the gift and respond.

The female protagonists of the story represent all disciples: they are present under the cross (Mk 15:40), as well as at the burial of Jesus (Mk 15:47); they followed him since the beginning of his preaching, known as the "Galilean spring"; unlike the disciples who all fled, they did not run away when faced with the cruel blow of their Master's passion and death. Now what they are about to experience is announced as a true and proper new beginning. It is indicated by the day in which the action takes place, which is the first day after the Sabbath and will come to be known as the eighth day. The hour is "very early . . . when the sun had risen," and not during the darkness. Truly, the rising sun inaugurates a new day, one that is bright and beautiful. The newness that the women are about to experience is made evident by the insistence on the stone that blocked the entrance to the tomb, which is mentioned twice (16:3–4) and described as "very large" (16:4). Nothing is said about who rolled it back, as if to suggest that something extraordinary and inexplicable had happened. After entering the tomb, the women see a mysterious figure, "a young man, dressed in a white robe, sitting on the right side" (16:5). It is not the Risen One, because the man says openly, "he is not here." It is not one of the disciples because they would have been easily recognized. Perhaps it is a messenger of God, an angel. Or perhaps, as some interpreters have suggested due to the catechumenal nature of Mark's Gospel, the description could allude to the baptismal symbolism of the white dress, symbol of new life, and of the dignity of the catechumen made new through the Son, who sits at the right hand of God in the splendor of glory. This would then be a reference to the baptism of the catechumens at the Easter Vigil, and, in any case, to the experience offered to the catechumen of newness of the life of the risen ones in the Risen One—an anticipation and guarantee of a future glorious life.

The experience of the women can be articulated in three stages. The first is their painful and fearful reaction at Jesus's absence, "He is not here!" Then they realize that someone inexplicably took their Master's body. This is followed by the sight of this mysterious young man in the tomb. After reassuring them, the young man tells the women who listen full of fear and astonishment, "Do not be alarmed!" In this, a true and proper kerygma resounds on the lips of the young man; that is, a proclamation of the death and resurrection of Jesus. "You are looking for Jesus of Nazareth, who was crucified. He has been raised; he is not here. Look, there is the place they laid him" (16:6). This is a profession of the paschal faith of Easter that must resound from the mouth of every candidate at baptism and of every person born again in Christ. Then, there is the sending forth: "But go, tell his disciples and Peter that he is going ahead of you to Galilee; there you will see him, just as he told you" (16:7). Those who are reborn in Christ in baptism must bear witness to him before all! The fact that the Lord goes before his followers to Galilee just as he had preceded them toward Jerusalem (see Mk 10:32), is a clear reference to their discipleship and to his closeness to the first disciples and those of every era. So now Jesus calls them to follow him to the place where it all began in the first days of his earthly mission. Hence, they have the certainty that they are never alone; the Master, risen and alive, will accompany them on their journey, preceding them along the way toward the fulfillment of the Father's plan until everything shall be accomplished.

The women flee in terror and say "nothing to anyone" (16:8). Mark helps us to comprehend their understandable reaction to the mystery that overcomes them; the fear and astonishment of the women point to the inexplicable newness of what they just experienced. Their silence, however, does not indicate emptiness, but an inexpressible fullness yet to be understood. The overabundance of life that touched the women is a sign of what must reach and touch all those who receive the Gospel throughout all the various places and epochs of history. The women open the way for the transforming experience of the catechumens who receive the life of the Risen Lord in their own life. The night of absence of their Beloved who lies in the tomb, and of the subconscious expectation that drove the women to the tomb, was transformed into amazement before the young man dressed in white . . . *That* night is no longer night—the light now shines.

An objective experience, a free and transforming decision

In what does this light of new life consist? The narrative structure underlying the first eight verses of chapter 16 of Mark helps us understand. Here, and in each account of the appearance of the Risen One, are three moments that flow from encountering him: *initiative from above*, *recognition* on the part of the recipients, and *mission*. It is the experience at the foundation of the call of every disciple of Jesus, crucified and victorious over death.

The initiative comes from God. In the paschal stories, the Risen One presents himself alive, "appearing" (see Acts 1:3). Note the Greek verb *ofte* used in 1 Corinthians 15:3–8 and Luke 24:34, which in the Old Testament is used to describe theophanies (see Gen 12:7; 17:1; 18:1; 26:2). In

Mark 16:1–8, the experience happens to the women amid their astonishment and fear; it is not born from within them. This demonstrates how the nature of the encounter with the Risen One is one of *objectivity*. It is something that happened to the disciples and women, something that *came* to them, not something that *became* within them. Their emotions of faith and love did not create their object; rather, the living Lord himself aroused this paschal faith of love. This applies to the call to faith in the risen Jesus in all times; it comes from the outside. It is not the result of flesh and blood, but of grace. It is a free gift that we gain by opening ourselves through freedom of the will.

And the role that freedom plays is shown in the paschal account through the gradual process of recognition. It was necessary for the first believers to believe by their own eyes and open themselves inwardly to what happened to the Lord Jesus. Their journey goes from astonishment and doubt to their profession of the risen Christ: "Then their eyes were opened, and they recognized him" (Lk 24:31). In his account, Mark emphasizes the fear and astonishment of the women, but clearly explains why. They understood that they had experienced something immeasurably beyond words, which commissions them to proclaim the resurrection of Jesus to the disciples and tell them that he would precede them to Galilee. This process of gradual recognition that moves from astonishment to missionary send-off through an act of revelation from on high, leads to a *subjective and interior type* of foundational experience of Christian faith. It further guarantees a free and voluntary consent in the story of each person who has faith in Christ and who follows him. The terror and amazement of the women, in other words, witnesses to human freedom in the face of what comes from above and asks to be received; no one may force the catechumen to have faith, for it is their decision to become involved.

And it is between the initiative from on high and its gradual recognition that the life-changing encounter takes place. Directly and with risk, the living Christ reaches his followers and animates them with new life, making them witnesses to him, who was victorious over death, and witnesses of that encounter with him that will forever mark their lives. "Go" were the words of the young man dressed in white to the women: "Go into all the world and proclaim the good news to the whole creation," were words of the final discourse of Mark's Gospel (Mk 16:15). The paschal experience, both objective and subjective, by the power of divine action embraced in human freedom, is profoundly *transformative*. From this experience a new creature is born, and the mission begins. And from it the Christian movement draws force and will spread to the ends of the earth.

Stopping at verse eight of chapter 16, as the original text of the evangelist presumably did, the story ends only to continue into life. Having been resurrected by the Father, Jesus sends his followers forth. He now desires to be proclaimed and encountered as a living Redeemer by every human being, in every age, and in every place. Inasmuch as Christians allow themselves to be touched by the living Christ, all the more will they be free from self, free for the Father, and free for others. They shall fulfill their vocation in the Church and in the world, stirring mankind toward freedom, opening the way to the coming kingdom.

In regard to the future of his mission, Jesus seems to see his followers as disciples called to freedom given from above, in order to become workers in the coming kingdom. Those who are truly free for the Father and for others live their vocation in the belief of the impossible possibility of God, which is revealed in Jesus Christ. Those who are free testify that freedom, even if defeated, merits being experienced. It is infectious and liberating, because, like the freedom of the Nazarene, it is a revelation and the gift of a greater mystery. The world will not be rid of the evil that oppresses it by the hardworking hands of people alone; there will be no deep and lasting liberation unless those same hands also open up in praise and invocation to receive the gift that comes from above. The emancipation of modern humanity, when it comes about solely by worldly efforts, serves only to produce every sort of totalitarianism and violence. The freedom that has been offered to history through Jesus Christ, who died and rose again, frees us from ourselves to make us live in love and hope for the Father and for others. And it makes our entire life a liturgy of praise to the Father and of service to others in the life-giving communion of the Church. Jesus, a free man, does not cease to rouse people to freedom!

We can then say, as M. Grilli explains, that "Mark's conclusion is open-ended because the reader is called to enter into the story and participate: to believe or not to believe. The life of Jesus recounted, the story of the crucified Messiah . . . is full of uncertainties and challenges. The reader is called to give an answer, or rather, to make a choice, to set out on the journey to meet Jesus on the roads of Galilee, that is, on the roads of life . . . or to reject the encounter and escape due to fear, indifference, or any other reason."[1] That which Mark is sure of, however, is that from the experience of the women at the empty tomb comes a message truly for all people, in every place and every age: "From now on, every human being can go

---

1. M. Grilli, *"Paradosso" e "mistero," Il vangelo di Marco* (Bologna, EDB, 2012), 114.

through the streets of their own 'Galilee' and build a
future for themselves and their children, without fear that
it will all end in a tomb."[2] In the narration of the Gospel of
Mark, the Gospel of the catechumen, the Gospel of the
night that illuminates all nights, we correspond less inade-
quately only by turning to the risen Jesus with words of
love that speak to him of the fullness of our free consent
and our humble, trusting decision to place ourselves
among his followers, with such words like these attributed
to Saint Augustine:

> Lord Jesus,
> May I know myself and know you,
> May I desire nothing but you.
> May I forget myself and love you.
> May I do everything only for you.
> May I humble myself and exalt you.
> May I think of nothing other than you.
> May I die to myself and live in you.
> May I accept whatever happens as from you.
> May I renounce myself in order to follow you,
>   and ever desire to follow you.
> May I fly from myself and take refuge in you,
>   so that I would be worthy to defend you.

---

2. Ibid., 115.

May I fear myself, and fear you,

    so that I will be among those chosen by you.

May I distrust myself and put my trust in you.

May I be willing to obey for your sake.

May I cling to nothing except to you,

    and may I be poor because of you.

Look upon me, that I may love you.

Call me that I may see you,

      so that I can forever enjoy you. Amen! [3]

---

3. *Oratio Sancti Augustini qua petitur intima Jesu Christi cognitio ac sequela*, in *Enchiridion Indulgentiarum* (Vatican City: Typis Polyglottis Vaticanis, 1952), no. 88.

A Journey That Continues

The fundamental option of Jesus of Nazareth, that which enlightens and maintains his journey, is his unconditional choice to love God and his kingdom. From this stems the total willingness of Jesus to give of himself for the salvation of mankind so that humanity's existence is fulfilled according to the plan that the Father has for each person and for humanity as a whole. This helps us to understand Mark's account, which presents the way Jesus conducts himself in key scenes of his life: in his baptism in the Jordan, his temptation in the desert, as well as in the description of a typical day in the Nazarene's Galilean ministry, known as the day of Capernaum.

The underlying option of the earthly life of the Son of God challenges the disciple and calls him to do the same. The freedom from self in order to live for the Father and for others is a rejection of selfishness and sin in whatever form they exist, as well as a humble, courageous, and clear choice to unconditionally belong to God and to his plan of salvation for everyone.

With regard to his life, Jesus calls us to purify our hearts from all our selfish and imprisoning attachments to this world in order to choose the road of love to the Father and to others by accepting the life-giving experience of forgiveness and grace. This alone frees us and changes lives. This is the purgative way.

The fundamental decision of the Galilean prophet was confirmed in the way he faced his destiny of suffering and death on the cross. We see this in his repeated proclamations of his passion, his experience of prayer and temptation in Gethsemane, and the account of his betrayal and final abandonment. At the prospect of his earthly end, Jesus overturns all human reasoning and expectation and confronts death solely according to the perspective of the divine plan and obedience to the Father. As Jesus lived for love, so he lays down his life for love in his ultimate and supreme surrender. And this is what the Master asks of the disciple; it is the choice that gives meaning to life, and, at the same time, will give meaning to death.

The one who strives to live in love of God and others in the example of and as a follower of Christ shall not regard death as the ultimate silence on the threshold of nothingness; rather, it shall be a blessed embrace with which the Lord of life shall receive his faithful servant into his bosom. To live is to learn how to die; those who live for love, shall die in the love of the living and holy God. Despite how dark the night of grief may seem or how obscure the passage of death may appear, those who choose, as the foundation of their decisions and life's work, union with the Father and service of others as followers of Jesus will be able to recognize the light that illuminates the night and makes of it an eternal dawn. This is the illuminative way.

The way in which the future mission of the Son of God unfolds becomes clear in Mark's brief account of the experience of the women at the tomb. Having risen from the dead, the Lord Jesus will not cease to take the initiative to visit and sustain his followers and to call all those who do not yet know him or believe in him to have faith in him. This action of the living Christ in the Spirit requires a free response from its recipients. And just like the women at the empty tomb, they, too, may know fear and astonishment. But it will be precisely in the crucible of discernment and decision that the recipients can either respond or not to the invitation to go and proclaim to others the message that transforms lives.

The experience of the encounter with Christ is objective in origin, because it comes above all from God through the proclamation of his Gospel and the illuminating work of the Spirit. It is subjective in its recipient, because the choice to believe will always remain the fruit of freedom that consents to the call and to the gift of grace. In each case, the encounter is a transformative event that does not leave people as they were. This is the unitive way.

A witness to this future transformative power of Jesus in people's lives is Mark himself. We see this in the title of his book: "The beginning of the good news of Jesus Christ, the Son of God" (Mk 1:1). Each of the terms of this formula contains a precise message.

In the biblical Greek, the first word *arché*, meaning "beginning," is not used in a merely temporal sense. Rather, it also means something that is foundational and indicates that what follows has meaning and value. Therefore, the evangelist wishes to communicate to his readers/listeners what he considers to be at the basis of everything: the *articulus stantis aut cadentis fidei* (the article on which faith stands or falls), that on which being a believer and disciple of the Lord Jesus stands or falls. His narrative does not, in fact, merely give information; rather, he wants to touch hearts, change lives, inflame, and feed the fire of the disciple's faith. Mark seeks to enliven that which he presents; he wants to establish an infectious

continuity between the word and life. He writes to communicate what he personally experienced, what forever
changed his heart, what is a true, new, and transformative
beginning.

What will produce such a transformation is indicated
by a term that has had an extraordinary destiny: *gospel*. In
and of itself, the word was not new. In the classical world,
gospel was used to indicate an important announcement
full of actual or hoped-for positive consequences. For
example, we have preserved in an inscription in Priene,
Turkey, dating from 9 B.C. the announcement of Emperor
Augustus's birthday, referred to as a gospel. In the Greek
translation of the Hebrew Bible, *bissar* is translated *euag-
gelion*, which means "to give the good news," as in Isaiah
52:7, "How beautiful upon the mountains / are the feet of
the messenger who announces peace, / who brings good
news, / who announces salvation." In the Letter to the
Romans, Paul uses the noun form to signify the center and
the heart of his message: "For I am not ashamed of the
gospel; it is the power of God for salvation to everyone
who has faith, to the Jew first and also to the Greek. For in
it the righteousness of God is revealed through faith for
faith; as it is written, 'The one who is righteous will live by
faith'" (Rom 1:16–17). Mark, however, is the first to make
an account of the good news. He created a kind of literary
genre of the life of Jesus presented as the "good news." He

did not want to write a biography or create a memoir in and of itself. His is the announcement or proclamation of what can forever change one's life into good; it is the "good news" that makes new and good according to the plan of God, opening us to God's future for us.

This Gospel is designated "of Jesus," followed by the double title, "Christ, the Son of God." In reality, Mark is already telling a rather decisive story of faith in this initial weighty formula. With the term, "Jesus," he refers to the earthly life of the Nazarene protagonist, and he will soon describe his works and what his days were like. With the expressions, "Christ, the Son of God," true and proper titles full of theological meaning, he is indicating the condition of Jesus as Messiah, anointed by God for his mission and equal to God by his nature as Son. "Jesus Christ, the Son of God" is, in fact, the account of the Nazarene's story, he who was humbled and exalted, crucified and resurrected, a man among men and the eternal Son who came to assume the human condition. He is the good news. The Christian proclamation is the story of Jesus, his teaching, the way he interacted with the people, how he liberated and healed, his union with the Father, the journey toward Jerusalem, the days of his passion, death, and resurrection, his experience, risen to life, who gives the Spirit and makes us sharers in divine life. The purpose of Mark is kerygmatic, that is, "to present Jesus as the Messiah and make sure that every person recognizes, believes, and is sustained by the faith that Christ is truly the decisive moment of history, in every person's story."[1]

The future to which the protagonist of the Gospel of Mark looks is our future . . . it is us, we who are reached by the proclamation of the good news and called to believe in the Gospel of Jesus Christ, the Son of God. This was also the experience of Mark from the moment in which the Lord Jesus entered his life. The evangelist proclaims the one he personally encountered. And it is he, the Risen One, who stands before us and speaks to us in the words of the second Gospel: he calls us to follow him; he invites us to participate in the divine life; he purifies us from evil and gives us the gift of freedom that does not disappoint; he enlightens us as to the meaning of our lives; he gives us sweetness in our consent to believe the truth. He stands at our door knocking. He asks us to open that door, which is locked from the inside, so he can come in and dine with us, sharing the bread of heaven (see Rev 2:17, 20). To him everyone shall give an answer. No one can take the place of another. Still, no one will remain alone who is ready to give their "yes." Jesus himself, living and glorious, will stay close, and with him his community, the Church of the

---

1. M. Grilli, *"Paradosso" e "mistero," Il vangelo di Marco,* op. cit., 17.

Gospel and of the sacraments, of faith and love. The conclusion of this journey is a new beginning, which leads one to offer words like these to the Lord Jesus, in faith and humble love:

> Christ,
> radiant image of the Father,
> Prince of Peace,
> who reconciles God to man
> and man to God,
> eternal Word made flesh,
> and flesh deified in the spousal encounter,
> in you alone
> we shall embrace God.
> You who became small
> to allow yourself to be seized by the thirst
> of our knowledge and our love,
> grant that we may seek you with desire,
> that we may believe in you during the darkness
>   of faith,
> that we may wait for you in ardent hope,
> love you in freedom
> and in our heart's joy.
> Do not let us be overcome
> by the power of darkness,
> or seduced by the glitter

of what passes away.

Give us, therefore, your Spirit,

so that he himself becomes in us

desire, faith,

hope, and humble love.

Then we shall search for you, Lord, in the night,

we shall keep watch for you in every era,

and the days of our mortal life

will become as a beautiful dawn,

in which you shall come,

bright morning star,

to be for us in the end

the Sun that knows no sunset.

Amen. Alleluia![2]

---

2. Bruno Forte, *Preghiere: Il mendicante del cielo* (Cinisello Balsamo: Edizioni San Paolo, 2007), 32ff.

About the Author

Bruno Forte was ordained to the priesthood in 1973 and named Archbishop of Chieti-Vasto, Italy, in 2004. A renowned theologian, Forte obtained his doctorate in theology at the Theological Faculty of Naples, Italy, and subsequently studied in Tübingen, Germany, and Paris, France.

In 2011, Pope Benedict XVI appointed him one of the founding members of the Pontifical Council for the Promotion of the New Evangelization. Forte is also a member of the Pontifical Council for Culture and the Pontifical Council for Christian Unity. For two five-year terms he was part of the International Theological Commission of the Holy See.

Widely published in Europe and Latin America, several of his books have been published in North America, including *The Trinity As History: Saga of the Christian God* (St Pauls/Alba House, 1989), *Why Go to Confession?: Reconciliation and the Beauty of God* (Pauline Books & Media, 2007), and *The Portal of Beauty: Towards a Theology of Aesthetics* (William B. Eerdmans Publishing Company, 2008).

BOOKS & MEDIA

A mission of the Daughters of St. Paul

As apostles of Jesus Christ, evangelizing today's world:

We are CALLED to holiness
by God's living Word and Eucharist.

We COMMUNICATE the Gospel message
through our lives and through all
available forms of media.

We SERVE the Church
by responding to the hopes and needs
of all people with the Word of God,
in the spirit of St. Paul.

For more information visit our Web site:
www.pauline.org.

Pauline
BOOKS & MEDIA

The Daughters of St. Paul operate book and media centers at the following addresses. Visit, call, or write the one nearest you today, or find us at www.pauline.org.

CALIFORNIA
3908 Sepulveda Blvd, Culver City, CA 90230   310-397-8676
935 Brewster Avenue, Redwood City, CA 94063   650-369-4230
5945 Balboa Avenue, San Diego, CA 92111   858-565-9181

FLORIDA
145 S.W. 107th Avenue, Miami, FL 33174   305-559-6715

HAWAII
1143 Bishop Street, Honolulu, HI 96813   808-521-2731
Neighbor Islands call: 866-521-2731

ILLINOIS
172 North Michigan Avenue, Chicago, IL 60601   312-346-4228

LOUISIANA
4403 Veterans Memorial Blvd, Metairie, LA 70006 504-887-7631

MASSACHUSETTS
885 Providence Hwy, Dedham, MA 02026   781-326-5385

MISSOURI
9804 Watson Road, St. Louis, MO 63126   314-965-3512

NEW YORK
64 W. 38th Street, New York, NY 10018   212-754-1110

PENNSYLVANIA
Philadelphia—relocating   215-676-9494

SOUTH CAROLINA
243 King Street, Charleston, SC 29401   843-577-0175

VIRGINIA
1025 King Street, Alexandria, VA 22314   703-549-3806

CANADA
3022 Dufferin Street, Toronto, ON M6B 3T5   416-781-9131

¡También somos su fuente para libros,
videos y música en español!